Science Questions

What Causes an Earthquake?

by Megan Cooley Peterson

Bullfrog
Books

Ideas for Parents and Teachers

Bullfrog Books let children practice reading informational text at the earliest reading levels. Repetition, familiar words, and photo labels support early readers.

Before Reading
- Discuss the cover photo. What does it tell them?
- Look at the picture glossary together. Read and discuss the words.

Read the Book
- "Walk" through the book and look at the photos. Let the child ask questions. Point out the photo labels.
- Read the book to the child, or have him or her read independently.

After Reading
- Prompt the child to think more. Ask: Earthquakes involve Earth's plates. Did you know about Earth's plates before reading this book? What more would you like to learn about Earth's layers?

Bullfrog Books are published by Jump!
5357 Penn Avenue South
Minneapolis, MN 55419
www.jumplibrary.com

Library of Congress Cataloging-in-Publication Data

Names: Peterson, Megan Cooley, author.
Title: What causes an earthquake? / by Megan Cooley Peterson.
Description: Minneapolis, MN: Jump!, Inc., [2024]
Series: Science questions | Includes index.
Audience: Ages 5–8
Identifiers: LCCN 2022049650 (print)
LCCN 2022049651 (ebook)
ISBN 9798885244879 (hardcover)
ISBN 9798885244886 (paperback)
ISBN 9798885244893 (ebook)
Subjects: LCSH: Earthquakes—Juvenile literature.
Classification: LCC QE534.3 .P48 2024 (print)
LCC QE534.3 (ebook)
DDC 551.22—dc23/eng20230123
LC record available at https://lccn.loc.gov/2022049650
LC ebook record available at https://lccn.loc.gov/2022049651

Editor: Jenna Gleisner
Designer: Emma Almgren-Bersie

Photo Credits: Tada Images/Shutterstock, cover; Xieyouding/iStock, 1; NOPPHARAT9889/Shutterstock, 3; Andrea Danti/Shutterstock, 4, 23tl, 23bl; Panther Media GmbH/Alamy, 5, 23br; Ningaloo.gg/Shutterstock, 6–7, 23tr; wavebreakmedia/Shutterstock, 10–11; Marti Bug Catcher/Shutterstock, 12; VisualProduction/Shutterstock, 13; hepatus/iStock, 14–15, 23tm; Nelson Antoine/Shutterstock, 16; Alter-ego/Shutterstock, 17; Pixel-Shot/Shutterstock, 18–19; shcherbak volodymyr/iStock, 20–21; Ekkaluck Sangkla/Shutterstock, 23bm; conzorb/Shutterstock, 24.

Printed in the United States of America at Corporate Graphics in North Mankato, Minnesota.

Table of Contents

Shake and Break

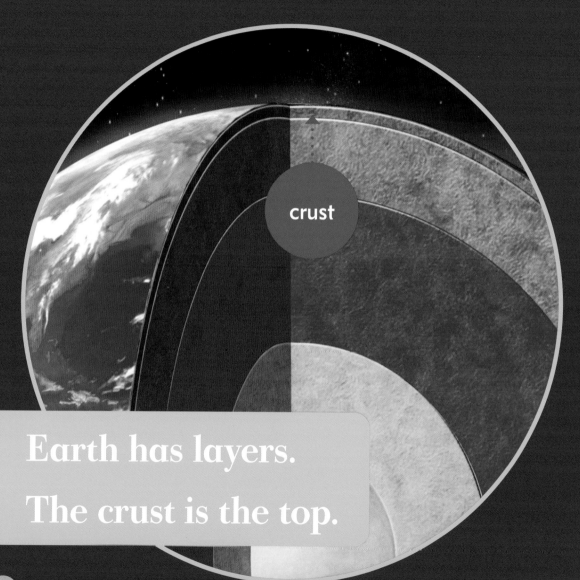

crust

Earth has layers.

The crust is the top.

It has pieces.
They are plates.

plate

They meet at fault lines.
They fit like a puzzle.

fault
line

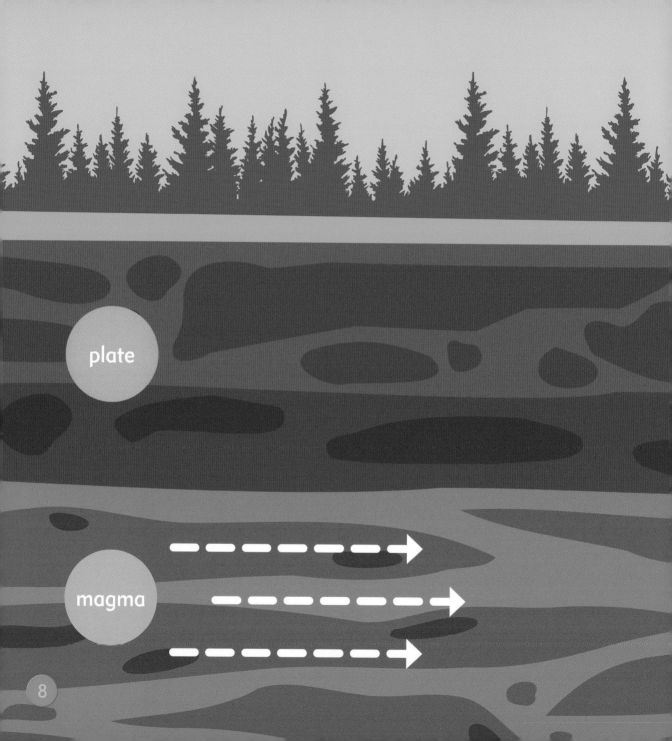

Magma is under them.

It is hot.

It flows.

Plates move on it.

We can't feel it.

Why?

They move slow.

Some push together.

They go up.

12

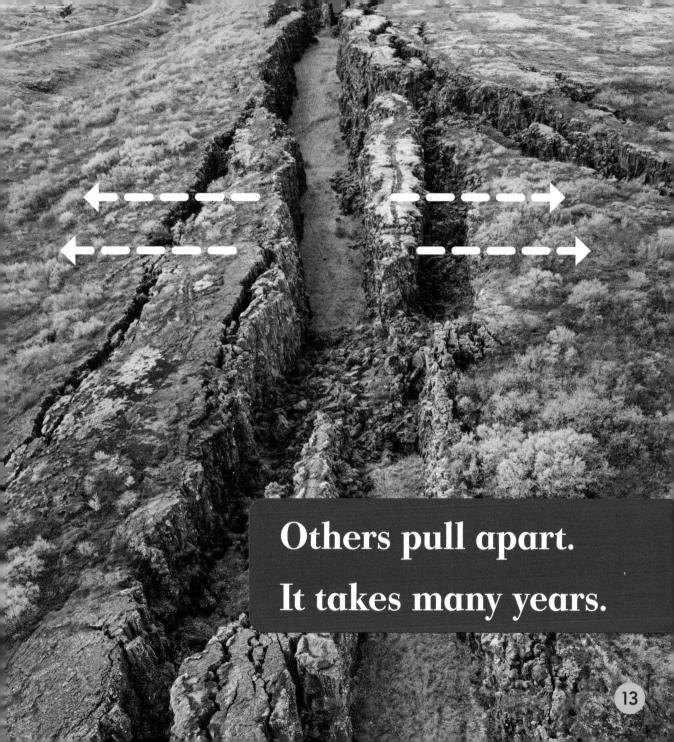

Others pull apart.
It takes many years.

Some slide past each other.
It makes energy.
The ground shakes.
Crack!
It breaks open.

Buildings shake.
Some break.
Watch out!

**Objects fall.
Oh, no!**

The plates lose energy.
The shaking stops.

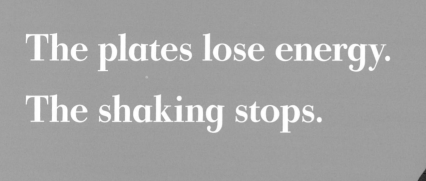

It is over.

We are safe.

We clean up.

How an Earthquake Happens

Earthquakes can happen when two plates push together, pull apart, or slide past each other. This happens at fault lines. Take a look!

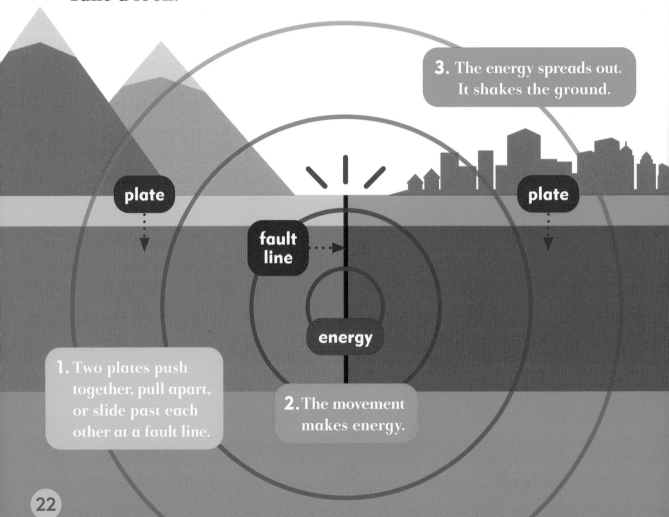

3. The energy spreads out. It shakes the ground.

plate

plate

fault line

energy

1. Two plates push together, pull apart, or slide past each other at a fault line.

2. The movement makes energy.

Picture Glossary

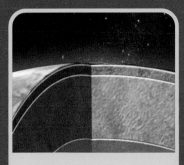

crust
The hard outer layer of Earth.

energy
The ability to do work or change things.

fault lines
Large breaks in Earth's surface.

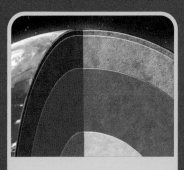

layers
Thicknesses laid under or over another.

magma
Melted rock beneath Earth's surface.

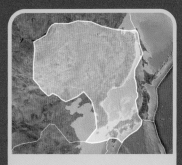

plates
Large, flat sheets of rock that make up Earth's crust.

Index

To Learn More

Finding more information is as easy as 1, 2, 3.

❶ Go to www.factsurfer.com

❷ Enter "whatcausesanearthquake" into the search box.

❸ Choose your book to see a list of websites.